LONDON'S BRIDGES

Stephen Croad

GENERAL EDITOR

Peter Fowler

ROYAL COMMISSION ON HISTORICAL MONUMENTS ENGLAND

LONDON HER MAJESTY'S STATIONERY OFFICE

© Crown copyright 1983
First published 1983

ISBN 0 11 701201 7

HER MAJESTY'S STATIONERY OFFICE

Government Bookshops

49 High Holborn, London WC1V 6HB
13a Castle Street, Edinburgh EH2 3AR
Brazennose Street, Manchester M60 8AS
Southey House, Wine Street, Bristol BS1 2BQ
258 Broad Street, Birmingham B1 2HE
80 Chichester Street, Belfast BT1 4JY

*Government Publications are also available
through booksellers*

SELECT BIBLIOGRAPHY

Howard Colvin, *A Biographical Dictionary of British Architects 1600-1840.* John Murray 1978
Eric de Maré, *London's Riverside.* Reinhardt 1958
Maurice Fitzmaurice, *Bridges.* London County Council 1906
Alan A. Jackson, *London's Termini.* David & Charles 1969
Peter Marsden, *Roman London.* Thames & Hudson 1980
Orleans House Gallery exhibition catalogue, *Richmond Bridge.* London Borough of Richmond upon
    Thames 1976
Geoffrey Phillips, *Thames Crossings.* David & Charles 1981
John Summerson, *Georgian London.* Penguin Books 1962
R.J.B. Walker, *Old Westminster Bridge.* David & Charles 1979
Charles Welch, *History of the Tower Bridge.* Smith, Elder & Co. 1894
H.P. White, *A Regional History of the Railways of Great Britain Vol. III Greater London.*
    David & Charles 1963

Printed in the UK for HMSO
Dd717098 C60 4/83

EDITOR'S FOREWORD

All the photographs in this book are held in the National Monuments Record (NMR), a national archive which is part of the Royal Commission on Historical Monuments (England). The NMR originated in 1941 as the National Buildings Record which, at a time when so much was being destroyed, took upon itself the task of photographing as many historic buildings as possible before it was too late. The Record continued its work after the War; its collection was transferred to the Royal Commission in 1963 as the core of the NMR. This now covers both architectural and archaeological subjects and contains well over a million photographs, together with maps, plans and other documents, relating to England's man-made heritage. The NMR is a public archive, open from 10.00 – 17.30 on weekdays; prints can be supplied to order on payment of the appropriate fee.

This book is the sixth of a series intended to illustrate the wealth of photographic material publicly available in the NMR. Many of the photographs are valuable in their own right, either because of their age or because they are the only records we now possess of buildings, and even whole environments, which have disappeared. Unlike other Commission publications, these are primarily picture-books, drawing entirely on what happens to be in the NMR. No attempt is made to treat each subject comprehensively nor to accompany it with a deeply researched text, but the text and captions are intended to give meaning to the photographs by indicating a context within which they can be viewed. It would be pleasing if they suggested lines of enquiry for others to follow. The titles in the series show where the strengths of the archive lie. Equally, of course, the collection is weak in some respects, and I hope that many of those who see this volume may be reminded of old, and perhaps disregarded, photographs of buildings and scenes in their possession. We would be glad to be told of the whereabouts of such photographs as potential contributions to the national record of our architectural and archaeological heritage.

The selection of photographs here is the first in this series to be limited to a particular place. London's river, as many have remarked before, both links and divides the nation's capital; the bridges, here arranged from east to west, provide the north-south link which holds it together astride the Thames. London without its bridges is unimaginable; yet for seventeen of its twenty centuries it made do with one (at most) and now the latest structure to span it, the flood barrier at Woolwich, is not a bridge at all. Maybe our suite of London's bridges is complete.

Royal Commission on Historical
Monuments (England),
Fortress House
23 Savile Row,
London W1X 1AB

Peter Fowler,
Secretary,
Royal Commission on
Historical Monuments (England);
General Editor,
NMR Photographic Archives

ACKNOWLEDGEMENTS

The Commission is grateful for permission to reproduce photographs
in the National Monuments Record of which the copyright is held
by:
Howarth-Loomes Collection
Museum of London
Oxfordshire County Libraries
The author would like to thank friends and colleagues, too numerous to
mention individually, who have assisted with the present work. Particular
thanks, however, are due to the photographic and order departments of the
RCHM, to the design and editorial departments at HMSO and to the
following: Frank Gardner, Bernard Howarth-Loomes, Ian Leith, Eric
Mercer, whose idea this originally was, and Michèle Millard. Priscilla
Boniface has contributed advice and encouragement throughout. Last, but
by no means least, the general editor, Dr Peter Fowler, has provided
guidance and assistance in no small measure.

(*front cover*) Chelsea Reach showing Battersea Bridge with Albert Bridge
and Chelsea Bridge downstream beyond. NMR, 1983.
(*frontispiece*) Waterloo Bridge from the Adelphi. Bedford Lemere, 1902.
(*opposite, above*) Arms of City of Westminster (*left*) and Borough of
Wandsworth (*right*).

London Bridge from a panorama by Jan Visscher, 1616.

LONDON'S BRIDGES

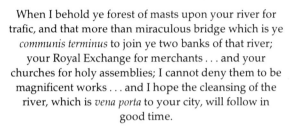

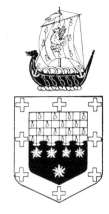

INTRODUCTION

When I behold ye forest of masts upon your river for
trafic, and that more than miraculous bridge which is ye
communis terminus to join ye two banks of that river;
your Royal Exchange for merchants . . . and your
churches for holy assemblies; I cannot deny them to be
magnificent works . . . and I hope the cleansing of the
river, which is *vena porta* to your city, will follow in
good time.

Sermon of the Bishop of London, 1620

The story of London can be seen as the
story of its great river, the Thames. From
the beginning, London was a centre for com-
munications by land and water, as ships from
the continent could reach this strategic inland
point by sailing up the Thames.

The following account traces, from the
earliest times, the history of attempts to bridge
the river's tidal reach. Today the tide flows to
Teddington Lock, but in the Roman period
the river may have been tidal only as far as
Chelsea and was probably fordable at Westminster at low tide.

The history of the City of London begins
with the establishment of a Roman town, for no
evidence that any settlement of significance
existed before the invasion by the armies of
Claudius in AD 43 has yet been discovered.
The most recent archaeological excavations
suggest that around AD 50 a planned town was
laid out on the north bank of the river and the
roads, when constructed, inevitably converged
on the crossing. To bridge the Thames the
Romans selected a spot where two spurs of
relatively high gravel land fairly close to the
river bank face one another. Until recently the
exact site of the bridge was unknown, but

excavations in 1981 uncovered what may be
the foundations of one of the piers of the
wooden bridge.

Documentary information about the first
thousand years of London's history is at best
scanty, and on the matter of London Bridge
non-existent until the early eleventh century.
It is reasonable to assume, however, that some
sort of structure existed throughout the period
after the Romans left; probably it was often
falling down. Meanwhile, the former Roman
establishment of *Londinium* became a permanent port and major town, surviving into and
then prospering in early medieval times. In
the 720s, the Venerable Bede called London 'a
mart of many peoples coming by land and sea'.

In 1091, a particularly bad storm caused the
river to flood sufficiently to sweep London
Bridge away. Weather in southern England
during the eleventh and twelfth centuries was
apparently subject to extremes; the antiquary
John Stow, writing at the end of the sixteenth
century, recorded that on 10 October 1114 the
river had dried up to the extent that 'a great
number of men, women and children did wade
over, both on horse and foot'. A reference to
the wooden bridge that existed in the 1170s

sheds light on London entertainments of the period for it mentions the suitability of the bridge as a vantage point for viewing water-tournaments.

In 1176 work was begun on the first stone bridge over the Thames, a structure which was to become a famous landmark. The bridge-master was Peter, Chaplain of St Mary's of Colechurch in the Poultry. He designed a bridge of twenty irregular pointed arches. The stone piers were laid within starlings (rubble-filled palisades constructed to protect the bridge from floating debris and collisions) on oak planks supported by timber piles, mostly of elm. The seventh opening from the south was not arched but contained a wooden draw-bridge, which was protected on the City side by a gatehouse. The bridge took over thirty years

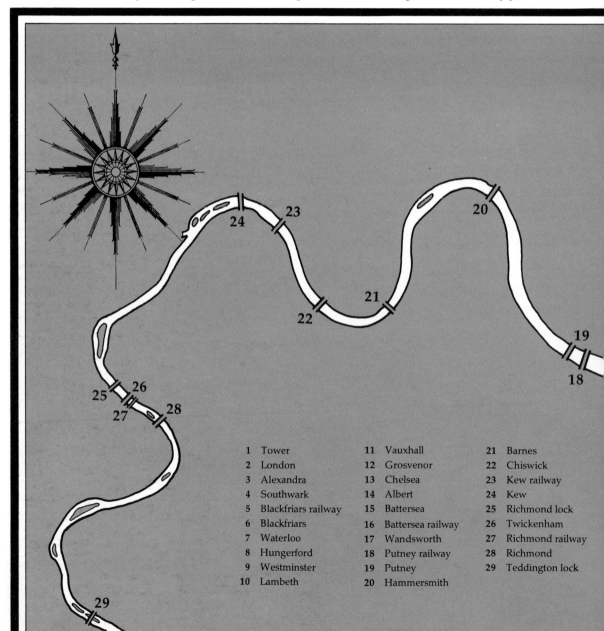

1	Tower	11	Vauxhall	21	Barnes
2	London	12	Grosvenor	22	Chiswick
3	Alexandra	13	Chelsea	23	Kew railway
4	Southwark	14	Albert	24	Kew
5	Blackfriars railway	15	Battersea	25	Richmond lock
6	Blackfriars	16	Battersea railway	26	Twickenham
7	Waterloo	17	Wandsworth	27	Richmond railway
8	Hungerford	18	Putney railway	28	Richmond
9	Westminster	19	Putney	29	Teddington lock
10	Lambeth	20	Hammersmith		

to build, being completed in 1209. Peter of Colechurch had died four years earlier and had been buried in the undercroft of the bridge chapel. Dedicated to St Thomas Becket, the chapel was the first building erected on the bridge, but it was envisaged that houses would also be built along it to produce revenue for its upkeep. The dwellings are clearly shown in John Norden's view of 1593, and Norden described the whole bridge as 'adorned with sumptuous buildings'.

Congestion on London Bridge was considerable and the only alternative methods of crossing the river were by boat or, the river being fairly clean, by swimming. An attempt was made in 1671 to increase the number of London's bridges to two when a bill was put forward for a bridge at Putney, but it was not

LONDON'S
BRIDGES

MILES
0   1   2   3

0   1   2   3
KILOMETRES

passed. On occasions, however, the Thames could be crossed without benefit of a bridge for it could ice over in places. On 9 January 1684, for example, during the Great Frost, the diarist John Evelyn crossed the ice from Westminster Stairs for dinner with the Archbishop of Canterbury at Lambeth Palace. At other times the Thames moved at great speed. Shooting the rapids between the piers of London Bridge was something to be attempted with caution. As Ray's *Proverbs* of 1737 commented: 'London Bridge was made for wise men to go over and fools to go under.'

Finally, after nearly seventeen hundred years of managing with only one permanent crossing, London's citizens permitted themselves the luxury of additional bridges across the tidal Thames. In 1729 a wooden bridge was constructed at Putney and an Act of Parliament authorized the building of a bridge at Westminster in 1736. How much the delay was due to the fact that the Archbishop of Canterbury owned the only horse-ferry (one large enough to carry horses and carts), or to the resistance of ferrymen who naturally did not wish to lose a lucrative living, is difficult to gauge. However, the monopoly of the ferrymen was then broken and the Archbishop was paid compensation of £3,000, perhaps because his horse-ferry upstream at Lambeth was too close to survive competition from its new neighbour.

For years it had been proposed that a stone bridge be built to link the Palace of Westminster and St Peter's Abbey on the north bank with new settlements on the routes to the south. The final designs for Westminster Bridge were prepared by Charles Labelye in 1734 though not without criticism of the employment of a foreigner for such an important task. The construction work attracted a great deal of attention, for a major bridge had not been built over any English river for more than a century. An interesting feature was the method of construction; for the first time in England, caissons were used. These caissons were large wooden boxes which were floated out to the pier positions and then sunk. The water was then pumped out and each pier was built inside the caisson up to water level. Fender piles were driven around the two larger piers during construction but otherwise foundations were not laid. Perhaps this was the cause of later problems: the central pier partly subsided when the bridge was nearly complete in 1747, understandably increasing the criticism of its designer. The bridge was not opened to the public until November 1750.

A competition was held in 1759 to decide on the best design for the next important crossing of the Thames. The winner was Robert Mylne, a young Scot recently arrived in London. The new bridge was erected at Blackfriars, between the already existing London and Westminster Bridges.

A number of other permanent crossings were built over the Thames in the eighteenth century. The towns and villages to the west of London did not want to risk losing trade increasingly centred on London, and many of them erected bridges over the Thames. Three bridges were constructed entirely of wood: Putney (1729), Kew (1758-9) and Battersea (1771-2). James Paine, better known as a country-house architect, designed the stone bridges at Richmond (1774-7) and Kew (1783-9).

In 1811 the pound lock at Teddington was opened; it still marks the limit of the tidal reach of the Thames. The construction of the lock was an early attempt to control the high tides, which by the nineteenth century were about ten feet above the levels in the Roman period. The population of London had already passed the million mark by 1811 and more traffic needed to cross the busy waterway. Not only were bridges built on new sites, but those already existing were rebuilt or adapted.

The first iron bridge over the Thames was constructed at Vauxhall in 1811-16; it was originally known as Regent's Bridge. Waterloo Bridge was also built at this time (1811-17) and that at Southwark a little later (1824-31);

both were designed by John Rennie. Rennie's last major work was to replace the medieval London Bridge. His design was executed after his death by his son.

Several bridges were built as speculative ventures by companies formed of people anxious to transport others to what they hoped would be money-spinning concerns on the other side of the river. The first two suspension bridges over the tidal Thames were in this category: Hammersmith Bridge was built because the developers hoped to build on the south bank, and Hungerford Bridge because market traders were hoping for better business for the nearby market. Neither venture proved as successful as their entrepreneurial owners had hoped; housing on the south side of Hammersmith Bridge is even now compara- tively sparse, and Hungerford Market closed because trade did not improve. Nonetheless, the latter bridge together with Blackfriars Bridge and London Bridge were used by an enormous number of people walking to work. That some bridges were underemployed, however, did not go unnoticed. *Building News* commented in 1874: 'Some of the bridges are overthronged, and . . . overweighted, while others appear hardly to serve any general purpose at all.'

Overcrowding in the City and the East End had never been more acute than in the first half of the nineteenth century. By 1836, when the first railway in London opened, the population of the capital had increased to about one and three-quarter million. The first railway bridge to cross the Thames in central London was Grosvenor or Victoria Bridge (1858-9), which enabled the London, Brighton & South Coast Railway to enter the West End. Eventually four southern railway companies sought both a City and a West End terminus and each time a new Act of Parliament had to be passed to authorize the construction of a river bridge. The entry of railway lines into the capital caused considerable bad feeling because many of the constructions displaced the poorest citizens from their dwellings, thereby increas-

ing the already large vagrant population. The groups of poor women and children huddling on the stone seats of London Bridge made a deep impression on the artist Gustave Doré. The railways were at least of benefit to the middle classes who could move into suburbs like Kennington, Clapham, Balham, Crystal Palace and Herne Hill. Already in 1849 *The Builder* reported: 'Those parties who can afford it are beginning to move off a little way into the country along the different lines of railway.' The speculative builder was just ahead of the new commuters. It frightened a visitor from France: 'Where, when, how will the continual growth, frightening in its speed, of London . . . come to an end?'

With the creation in 1889 of the London County Council it was formally recognized that London had long since outgrown its political boundaries. Previously, Westminster and even the Tower of London had technically been in the county of Middlesex. In 1889 the new county of London extended upstream on the north bank to Hammersmith and also incorporated parts of Kent and Surrey.

Before 1889 vast public works had been undertaken to improve the capital. The Com- mission for Metropolitan Improvements and the chief engineer of the Metropolitan Board of Works, Sir Joseph Bazalgette, were respon- sible for the construction of the Thames Embankment, thereby giving new highways on both banks of the river. New bridges were an inevitable result. Chelsea suspension bridge was erected in 1851-8 to the design of Thomas Page, engineer of the new Westminster Bridge (1854-62). After more than thirty years' discussion, the Lambeth suspension bridge was built in 1862 close to Lambeth Palace, replacing the ancient ferry. The memory of it is perpetuated today by Horseferry Road from Victoria to the bridge.

Originally all but two bridges – London and Westminster – had been privately owned and tolls were levied as a means of offsetting the cost of construction and of financing upkeep.

These charges caused considerable ill-feeling: one of the acts of the Gordon rioters in 1780, for example, had been to burn down the toll-houses on Blackfriars Bridge. Five years later the Government bought out the owners and passage over the bridge became free. The Metropolitan Toll Bridges Act, 1877, enabled the Board of Works to buy the remaining bridges and free them from toll. This the Board proceeded to do over the next few years. The last bridge to levy tolls was the footbridge over Richmond Lock (1894). There, the charge of one penny was suspended during the Second World War and never re-introduced.

The most recent crossing of the Thames in central London on a new site was Tower Bridge, completed in 1894. It was the first bridge to be constructed downstream from London Bridge. Although many proposals had been put forward for a river crossing in the busy dockland area, the erection of a bridge over that part of the river raised numerous problems not previously encountered. It was, for example, necessary to allow for the passage of tall ships beneath the bridge. Horace Jones, City Engineer, first suggested a bascule bridge in 1878. The City Corporation eventually agreed to this idea and the Act of Parliament to authorize the construction of Tower Bridge was passed in 1885. The design of the bridge was influenced by the Government, which insisted that the style should be sympathetic to that of the Tower of London. Another condition, that the bridge should be armed with cannon, was later abandoned. V.S. Pritchett writing in *London Perceived* (1962) describes the bridge and its creator: 'Asked to build an epoch-making suspension bridge that shall be drawbridge as well, he builds – in the nineteenth century – something like a medieval castle of granite, . . . at the peak point of London's power and modernity, he creates a bridge suitable for King Arthur, the Black Prince, the archers at Agincourt, and operators

of the culverin; in order, one supposes, to disguise from himself the fact that he had really built a masterpiece of engineering.'

During the latter part of the nineteenth century and throughout the twentieth century the inner city population declined. More people preferred to live on the outskirts of the city or beyond and travel in to work. As the distances separating home and work grew, road transport played an increasingly important part in getting Londoners to and from their jobs. The vast increase in traffic resulted in the alteration of every one of London's road bridges. Vauxhall Bridge was rebuilt and Blackfriars Bridge was widened, both early in the twentieth century, to accommodate tramways. The Great Chertsey Road, one of a number of new arterial roads opened in the 1920s and 1930s, necessitated the erection of three new Thames bridges. Two of them, Chiswick and Twickenham, were within the tidal reach. They were opened, with Hampton Court Bridge, on 3 July 1933, by the Prince of Wales.

Lambeth, Chelsea, Waterloo, and Wandsworth bridges were all rebuilt in the 1930s. London Bridge had been widened in 1902-4, but it could not cope with the increase in traffic that followed the Second World War. The decision to rebuild again was taken, but because over 70,000 pedestrians crossed the river here daily, the work was carried out while the bridge remained in use. This newest London Bridge, begun in 1968, was completed in 1972.

Londoners perhaps do not always recognize the achievement that their bridges represent. A Frenchman commenting on Tower Bridge in particular and the English in general was less reticent: 'No other people know how to unite with the same harmonious force the cult of the past, the religion of tradition, to an unchecked love of progress and a lively and insatiable passion for the future.'

TOWER BRIDGE.

The first bridge to be built downstream from London Bridge and still the last before the sea. With its double-leaf bascule, it is the only movable bridge on the river, designed to allow tall ships to enter the Upper Pool of London. Tower Bridge was built by Sir John Wolfe-Barry as engineer and Sir Horace Jones as architect. Work began in 1886 and the bridge was opened amid great festivities by the Prince of Wales, later Edward VII, on 30 June 1894. To minimize the risk of failure, the engineering systems of the bridge were in duplicate. The bascules, each weighing over 1,000 tons, were originally raised by hydraulic power, but converted in recent years to electricity. Before the First World War about 100 people were employed in operating and maintaining Tower Bridge.

1 Appearing like the drawbridge of some medieval castle, the arches at each end of the bridge provide the supports for the suspension chains. From a stereoscopic card, *c.*1900. Copyright Howarth-Loomes Collection.

2 Under construction; the steel frame may be seen clearly. Unknown photographer, *c*.1889.

3 (*opposite*) Tower Bridge, nearly complete, seen from the Tower of London. Unknown photographer, *c*.1893.

4 (*overleaf*) From the south-east, showing in the foreground the works paddle-tug on standby for possible emergencies. Unknown photographer, *c*.1900.

5 LONDON BRIDGE.
The first permanent crossing of the tidal River Thames was constructed by the Romans sometime after AD 43. These remains, excavated in 1981, may be the foundations of one of the piers of that first London Bridge.
Jon Bailey, Department of Urban Archaeology, 1981. Copyright Museum of London.

6 LONDON BRIDGE.
The great bridge, designed by Peter of Colechurch, and built 1176-1209, was one of the wonders of the medieval world. It was thought that the last remnants of the bridge had been swept away before the advent of photography, but in 1921 when Adelaide House at the north end of the bridge was demolished one of the pointed stone arches of the original structure was uncovered.
Campbell's Press Studio, 1921.

LONDON BRIDGE.

The medieval bridge had been repaired and strengthened at various times throughout the eighteenth century, but in March 1821 the engineer John Rennie advocated the building of a new bridge. He died in October 1821 and a competition was held in 1823 to decide upon a design for the new work. More than one hundred entries were submitted but none was considered entirely satisfactory and Rennie's original design was eventually executed under the direction of his son, also named John, who was knighted on the completion of the work. The foundation stone was laid in 1825 and the opening ceremony was performed by King William IV and Queen Adelaide on 1 August 1831.

7 From a stereoscopic card, 1870s.
Copyright Howarth-Loomes Collection.

8 From a stereoscopic card, 1880s.
Copyright Howarth-Loomes Collection.

LONDON BRIDGE.
Rennie's London Bridge was widened in 1902-4 but proved inadequate for modern traffic. It was eventually decided to rebuild and the fabric of Rennie's bridge was sold for £1 million and re-erected at Lake Havasu City, Arizona, U.S.A., in 1970-1. The present London Bridge was designed by the City engineer, H.K. King, together with Mott, Hay & Anderson and the architects William Holford & Partners. The contractors were John Mowlem & Co. Work began in 1967 and the bridge was opened by Her Majesty the Queen on 16 March 1973.

9 (*opposite*) London Bridge photographed during the early twentieth-century widening. Unknown photographer, *c*.1903.

10 (*above*) The present London Bridge. NMR, 1982.

ALEXANDRA BRIDGE.
An Act of Parliament was passed in 1861 to allow a railway station in Cannon Street. The station, river bridge and approach viaducts were all designed by Sir John Hawkshaw, consulting engineer to the South Eastern Railway. Work commenced in July 1863 and Cannon Street Station opened on 1 September 1866.

11 (*opposite, top*) Showing the original overhead gantry signal box. Philip Norman Collection, 1870s.

12 (*opposite, bottom*) In the 1890s the bridge was widened to accommodate extra tracks. Philip Norman Collection, *c.*1900.

SOUTHWARK BRIDGE.
In 1813 a company was formed to provide a bridge at Southwark and it appointed John Rennie as engineer. Rennie built a bridge of three flat segmental arches of cast-iron designed to allow the greatest possible waterway. The project, begun in 1815, constituted the largest cast-iron structure then built. The bridge was illuminated with lamps and declared open at midnight on 24 March 1819. Demolition of old Southwark Bridge began in 1913 and the replacement was designed by the engineer Basil Mott of Mott, Hay & Anderson and the architect Sir Ernest George. Work was delayed during the First World War and Southwark Bridge was eventually opened by King George V on 6 June 1921.

13 (*above*) Rennie's cast-iron bridge. Unknown photographer, *c.*1910.

14 (*overleaf*) The present bridge photographed soon after completion. S.O. Gorse, *c.*1922.

BLACKFRIARS RAILWAY BRIDGE.
The City extension of the London, Chatham &
Dover Railway reached the south bank of the
Thames in 1864. There was a delay in crossing
the river because the City Corporation failed to
decide on a design for a bridge, but Joseph
Cubitt completed the work on 21 December
1864. Stones from the old Westminster Bridge,
demolished in 1861, were used in the abutments.

15 The arms of the railway company in cast-
iron on the bridge parapet. NMR, 1982.

16 Blackfriars road bridge from beneath the
railway bridge. NMR, 1982.

17 (*opposite*) The cast-iron piers of the railway
bridge. NMR, 1982.

BLACKFRIARS BRIDGE.
A competition to design a new bridge at Blackfriars was held in 1759 and the winner from sixty-nine entries was Robert Mylne. The bridge, originally known as Pitt Bridge, was opened on 19 November 1769. Mylne's bridge was demolished in 1860 and a temporary bridge erected. The foundation stone of a new structure, the present Blackfriars Bridge, designed by Joseph Cubitt, was laid in 1865. It was opened by Queen Victoria in 1869 on the same day that she opened Holborn Viaduct.

18 A rare photograph of the original Blackfriars Bridge. From a stereoscopic card, *c.*1860. Copyright Howarth-Loomes Collection.

19 (*opposite, top*) The present bridge, almost new. H.W. Taunt, *c.*1870. Copyright Oxfordshire County Libraries.

20 (*opposite, bottom*) View from the north bank. Campbell's Press Studio, *c.*1900.

WATERLOO BRIDGE.

John Rennie was asked to prepare designs for a new bridge in 1809. This was to be the first of three bridges he designed for the Thames in central London. When the foundation stone was laid, on 11 October 1811, the bridge was known as Strand Bridge. It was re-named in 1816 and the bridge was opened by the Prince Regent on 18 June 1817, the second anniversary of the Battle of Waterloo. In 1882-4 work was carried out to protect the foundations, but in 1923 three of the piers were found to be sinking; the bridge was closed in June 1934 and demolition started at once.

21 View from the south before the building of the embankments. Roger Fenton, *c*.1857.

22 (*opposite*) From beneath the arches of Somerset House. Unknown photographer, *c*.1860.

23 (*overleaf*) Showing the shot-tower on the south bank. H.W. Taunt, *c*.1880. Copyright Oxfordshire County Libraries.

WATERLOO BRIDGE.

The new concrete bridge was built to the designs of Sir Giles Gilbert Scott in conjunction with the engineers Rendel, Palmer & Tritton. Although work began in 1937, the official foundation stone was not laid until 4 May 1939. The bridge was opened to pedestrians and traffic in two lanes in 1942 and completed two years later.

24 Demolition work just beginning on Rennie's bridge. P.E.W. Street, 31 July 1934.

25 The temporary bridge and foundations for the new work, Campbell's Press Studio, c.1938.

26 The present bridge from the south bank. NMR, 1982.

HUNGERFORD BRIDGE.

A suspension bridge designed by Isambard Kingdom Brunel was built to provide a pedestrian link between the Hungerford Market and the south bank. Begun in 1841, Hungerford Bridge was opened on 1 May 1845. The market was eventually closed and the site sold for the proposed Charing Cross railway station. Demolition of the bridge followed, the suspension chains being sold for £5,000 to complete Brunel's more famous bridge at Clifton, Bristol, in 1864. Work on the Charing Cross railway bridge began in June 1860 to the designs of John Hawkshaw. The new iron girder structure, which made use of the brick piers of Brunel's bridge, was completed in 1864.

27 (*opposite*) Hungerford suspension bridge from the north bank. From a stereoscopic card, 1850s. Copyright Howarth-Loomes Collection.

28 (*overleaf*) Hungerford railway bridge, showing the bridges at Westminster and Lambeth beyond. Campbell's Press Studio, c.1920.

WESTMINSTER BRIDGE.

The first bridge after London Bridge to be built across the Thames in central London was designed by Charles Labelye, who submitted his plans in 1734 and was appointed 'engineer' in 1738. The first stone was laid on 29 January 1738/9 and the bridge was opened in November 1750. When in 1831 old London Bridge was removed, the greater scour of the river upstream undermined the foundations of Westminster Bridge and it became dangerous. Designs for a new structure were made by Thomas Page and work began in 1854. The present Westminster Bridge was opened on 25 May 1862.

29 A rare glimpse of the old bridge just before demolition and before the completion of Big Ben clocktower. Roger Fenton, *c.*1857.

30 (*opposite, bottom*) View from upstream on the Albert Embankment. NMR, 1980.

31 (*above*) Westminster Bridge decorated for the coronation of King Edward VII. Unknown photographer, 1902.

32 (*right*) Showing St Thomas's Hospital in the background. Campbell's Press Studio, 1930s.

LAMBETH BRIDGE.
The Act of Parliament authorizing the erection of a suspension bridge to replace the ancient horse-ferry at Lambeth was passed in 1861. The bridge was designed by P.W. Barlow and opened in November 1862. It cost less than £50,000 to build and by 1887 its condition was so serious that major repairs had to be carried out under the direction of Sir Benjamin Baker. The decision to rebuild completely was taken only five years later. Nothing was done and in 1905 a weight limit was imposed on vehicles using the bridge and gates were erected at each end to regulate the number of pedestrians. Despite the early decision to replace Lambeth Bridge, the old structure remained in use until 1929.

33 (*opposite*) Looking across the bridge towards Lambeth. Unknown photographer, *c*.1910.

34 (*above*) View from upstream showing Westminster Abbey and the Houses of Parliament. Henry Dixon & Son, 1912.

35 (*overleaf*) Unloading bricks at Millbank. H. W. Taunt, *c*.1880. Copyright Oxfordshire County Libraries.

LAMBETH BRIDGE.

The new bridge was designed by the engineer Sir George Humphreys with G. Topham Forrest and Sir Reginald Blomfield as architectural consultants. Work began in 1929 and the bridge was opened by King George V and Queen Mary on 12 July 1932.

36 (*opposite, top*) The temporary foot-bridge alongside the old suspension bridge. Photographed for Dorman, Long & Co., 1929.

37 (*opposite, bottom*) View from upstream – compare with Pl. 34. Campbell's Press Studio, c.1950.

VAUXHALL BRIDGE.

This, the first iron bridge over the Thames, was originally known as Regent's Bridge. The foundation stone was laid on 9 May 1811 and the bridge was opened on 4 June 1816. The design was by James Walker. In 1895 an Act was passed to rebuild the bridge, and demolition began in September 1898. A temporary bridge was erected and work on the new structure did not begin until 1904. It was eventually opened by the Prince of Wales on 26 May 1906. The Chief Engineer of the London County Council, Sir Maurice Fitzmaurice, designed the present Vauxhall Bridge, but modifications were made by the architects W.E. Riley and Richard Norman Shaw.

38 (*top*) James Walker's original iron bridge. E.J. Wallis, c.1890.

39 (*centre*) Construction work on the new bridge. Campbell's Press Studio, 1906.

40 (*bottom*) Two of the eight statues designed by Frederick Pomeroy and Alfred Drury. NMR, 1980.

41 (*overleaf*) GROSVENOR BRIDGE.
Grosvenor Bridge, also known as Victoria Bridge, was the first railway bridge to cross the Thames in the central London area. It was built to the designs of John Fowler for the London, Brighton & South Coast Railway. Work began on 9 June 1859 and the first train passed over it exactly one year later. Sir Charles Fox added a new bridge alongside to the east in 1865-6 and another was constructed downstream in 1907. The whole was rebuilt by Freeman, Fox & Partners between 1963 and 1967. NMR. 1982.

CHELSEA BRIDGE.
Chelsea suspension bridge was one of the achievements of the Commission for Metropolitan Improvements. Work commenced in September 1851 to the design of Thomas Page and the bridge was opened in March 1858 by the Prince Consort and the Prince of Wales. Extra chains were added by Sir Joseph Bazalgette in 1880 to support heavier loads. Demolition of Page's bridge began in 1935 and a replacement by Rendel, Palmer & Tritton to the designs of Sir Peirson Frank was begun in 1936. The opening ceremony was performed by the Prime Minister of Canada, W.L. Mackenzie King, on 6 May 1937.

42 Looking across the bridge and showing the toll houses. From a stereoscopic card, 1860s. Copyright Howarth-Loomes Collection.

43 (*opposite, top*) From upstream with the Grosvenor railway bridge beyond. Campbell's Press Studio, *c.*1910.

44 (*opposite, bottom*) The present bridge from downstream. Campbell's Press Studio, *c.*1940.

ALBERT BRIDGE.

The Act of Parliament permitting the construction of a new bridge was passed in 1864. However, there were long delays before work started and the Albert Bridge was not opened until September 1873. Designed by Roland Mason Ordish, it was originally a cantilever bridge, each half being supported by sixteen straight bars radiating from the tops of the towers. In 1884 the bridge was strengthened by Sir Joseph Bazalgette, whose modifications made it more like a conventional suspension bridge. In July 1973 the bridge was re-opened to light traffic following the construction of two river piers supporting the weight of the central span.

45 View from the north bank. Campbell's Press Studio, *c*.1950.

46 (*opposite*) View from the south bank. NMR, 1980.

BATTERSEA BRIDGE.

The timber bridge of 1771-2 was built by John Phillips under the direction of the young Henry Holland, then working for his father's building firm at Fulham. Originally of nineteen spans, four of the spans were later thrown into two. This bridge was to be made famous by the paintings of James Whistler, who lived for a number of years in Chelsea. A new Battersea Bridge was begun in 1886 and opened by the 5th Earl of Rosebery on 21 May 1890. The work was carried out by John Mowlem & Co. to the designs of Sir Joseph Bazalgette.

47 The wooden bridge photographed from the tower of Chelsea Old Church. Philip Norman Collection, c.1860.

48 The present bridge from upstream. NMR, 1982.

50 (opposite) Looking across the river to Chelsea. H.W. Taunt, c.1885. Copyright Oxfordshire County Libraries.

49 BATTERSEA RAILWAY BRIDGE.
The West London Extension Railway Bridge was jointly owned by the London & North-Western and the Great Western Railway Companies, each with one-third share, together with the London & South-Western Railway and the London, Brighton & South Coast Railway, with one-sixth share each. It was designed by Benjamin Baker and T.H. Bertram. The Act permitting it was passed in 1859 and the bridge opened on 2 March 1863. Built by Brassey & Ogilvie, it carried both Great Western broad gauge and London & North-Western standard gauge tracks. NMR, 1980.

51 WANDSWORTH BRIDGE.
The first Act of authorization was passed in 1864 and time extensions were granted in 1867 and 1870. Designed by J.H. Tolme, Wandsworth Bridge was eventually opened on 27 September 1873. It was of the continuous lattice girder type. In 1935 Sir Peirson Frank's design for a new bridge was approved and rebuilding was completed on 20 September 1940. NMR, 1980.

52 PUTNEY RAILWAY BRIDGE.
Designed by W. H. Thomas and W. Jacomb for the London & South-Western Railway. Authorized in 1886 and begun the following year, the first trains to cross the river on the Wimbledon and Putney branch of the London & South Western Railway ran on 3 June 1889. NMR, 1980.

PUTNEY BRIDGE.
Thomas Phillips built the wooden bridge according to a scheme provided by Dr William Cheselden, surgeon of St Thomas's Hospital. The Bill of authorization was passed by Parliament in 1726 and work was begun in March 1729. The bridge was opened on 14 November in the same year. A wider central span was created in 1871-2 by the removal of two piers and the erection of an iron centre resting on cast-iron cylinders.

53 Showing the aqueduct belonging to the Chelsea Waterworks Co. which formerly occupied the site of the present bridge. Unknown photographer, *c.*1880.

54 (*opposite, top*) Toll-house at the south end of Putney Bridge. Newton & Co., *c.*1880.

55 (*opposite, bottom*) Looking across the river to Putney. H.W. Taunt, *c.*1875. Copyright Oxfordshire County Libraries.

56 (*overleaf*) Toll-house and bridge piers photographed at low tide. Unknown photographer, *c.*1880.

PUTNEY BRIDGE.
A new bridge to the designs of Sir Joseph Bazalgette was built slightly upstream of the old. Begun in 1882, it was opened by the Prince and Princess of Wales on 29 May 1886.

57 (*opposite, top*) The bridge crowded, probably to view the start of the annual University boat race. H.W. Taunt, *c*.1895. Copright Oxfordshire County Libraries.

58 (*opposite, bottom*) Mudlarking at low tide. Herbert Felton, *c*.1940.

59 HAMMERSMITH BRIDGE.
The first suspension bridge over the Thames was designed by William Tierney Clark. The Act authorizing its construction was passed in 1824 and the foundation stone was laid the following year. The opening ceremony was held on 8 October 1827. Newton & Co., *c*.1880.

HAMMERSMITH BRIDGE.

The new suspension bridge begun in November 1884 and based upon the foundations of the previous bridge was designed by Sir Joseph Bazalgette and opened by Prince Albert Victor, Duke of Clarence, on 18 June 1887. Meanwhile a crossing was provided by a temporary bridge, the materials of which were re-used for the Teddington footbridge. In 1973 the Greater London Council strengthened Hammersmith Bridge at a cost of £900,000.

60 (*opposite*) Looking across the bridge. H.W. Taunt, *c.*1895. Copyright Oxfordshire County Libraries.

61 (*above*) View from the south bank. Campbell's Press Studio, *c.*1910.

62 (*opposite, top*) BARNES BRIDGE.
This bridge, built to carry the Richmond and Hounslow loop line of the London & South-Western Railway, was designed by Joseph Locke and Thomas Brassey and opened on 22 August 1849. It was partially reconstructed in 1891-5 when overhead girders were erected to the design of Edward Andrews. NMR, 1980.

CHISWICK BRIDGE.
The Act of Parliament authorizing a new bridge at Chiswick was passed in 1928 as part of a major road building scheme. Designed by Sir Herbert Baker with Alfred Dryland as engineer, the bridge is of ferro-concrete faced with Portland stone. Chiswick Bridge was the first of three bridges on the Great Chertsey Road opened by the Prince of Wales on 3 July 1933.

63 (*opposite, bottom*) View from downstream. NMR, 1982.

64 (*below*) The bridge under construction. Unknown photographer, *c.*1931.

KEW RAILWAY BRIDGE.

The London & South-Western Railway Company obtained powers in 1864 to extend the line from South Acton Junction to Richmond. The lattice girder bridge at Kew was designed by W.R. Galbraith and built by Brassey & Ogilvie. It was opened on 1 January 1869.

65 Showing Strand on the Green beyond. NMR, 1982.

66 (*below*) From beneath the bridge showing the cast-iron piers. NMR, 1982.

67 (*opposite, top*) From downstream at low tide. NMR, 1982.

KEW BRIDGE.

John Barnard designed the eleven-span wooden bridge which was built at Kew in 1758-9. The proprietor was Robert Tunstall of Brentford, whose family had owned the horse-ferry at Kew for over a century. In 1782 Robert Tunstall junior initiated legislation to allow him to build a new bridge of stone downstream of the old. This, designed by James Paine, was completed on 22 September 1789 and opened with a procession led by King George III. In 1898 an Act was passed to replace Paine's bridge. The new bridge, built by Easton Gibb to the designs of Sir John Wolfe-Barry and C.A. Brereton, was opened on 20 May 1903 by the King, who named it the King Edward VII Bridge.

68 From upstream on the Kew Gardens bank. H.W. Taunt, *c.*1885. Copyright Oxfordshire County Libraries.

69 Showing the tower of Kew Bridge pumping station on the north bank. Unknown photographer, *c.*1895.

70 The present bridge from upstream. NMR, 1980.

71 (*opposite*) The centre arch. NMR, 1980.

72 RICHMOND LOCK.
Permission to construct a lock and weir at Richmond was granted in 1890 after many years of petitioning and the opportunity was taken to build a footbridge at the same time. The work was directed by the engineer of the Thames Conservancy, James More, and the bridge was opened by the Duke and Duchess of York on 19 May 1894. It was the last bridge on the tidal river to levy tolls. H.W. Taunt, *c.*1895. Copyright Oxfordshire County Libraries.

73 TWICKENHAM BRIDGE.
This was the second of the three bridges on the
Great Chertsey Road opened on the same day,
3 July 1933, by the Prince of Wales. The others
were at Chiswick and Hampton Court. Twickenham Bridge, begun on 1 June 1931, was designed
by Maxwell Ayrton with Alfred Dryland as
engineer. It is of reinforced concrete and the
three river arches have permanent hinges for self-
adjustment. It was the first large concrete bridge
in the country to be constructed on this principle.
NMR, 1980.

RICHMOND RAILWAY BRIDGE.
Originally named the Richmond, Windsor and Staines Railway Bridge, it was designed by Joseph Locke for the
London & South-Western Railway and opened in 1848. The present bridge is a reconstruction of 1906-8 by
J.W. Jacomb-Hood, chief engineer of the London & South-Western Railway, and the Horseley Bridge Company.

74 (*opposite, top*) View from upstream at Richmond. London, Midland & Scottish Railway Collection, 1890.

75 (*opposite, bottom*) View from downstream showing Richmond beyond. H.W. Taunt, *c.*1895. Copyright Oxfordshire
County Libraries.

76 (*below*) Showing Twickenham Bridge and Richmond Lock beyond. NMR, 1982.

77 (*overleaf*) Photographed from Twickenham Bridge. NMR, 1982.

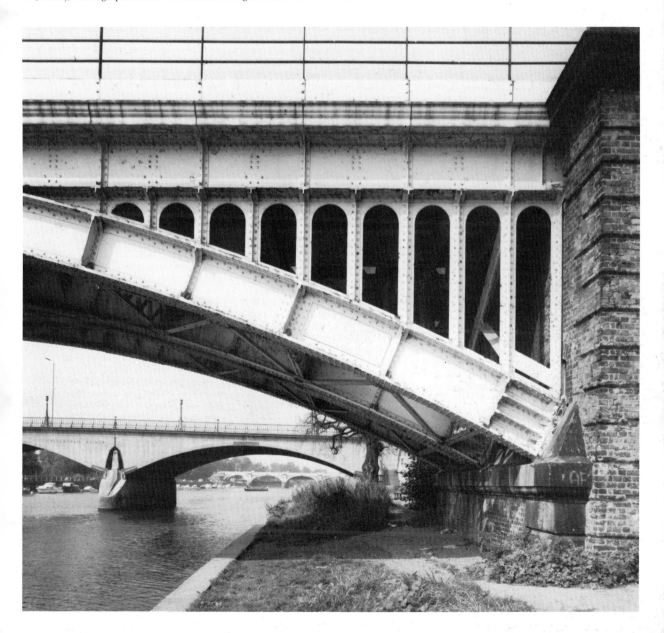

RICHMOND BRIDGE.
Designed by Kenton Couse and James Paine, Richmond Bridge was built 1774-7. The construction was financed in an unusual way on the tontine principle and the last annuitant survived until 1859. In 1937 work began on widening the bridge on the upstream side and this was completed in the summer of 1939.

78 View of the upstream side before widening. From a stereoscopic card, 1860s. Copyright Howarth-Loomes Collection.

79, 80 (*opposite and inset*) The upstream side showing the reset datestone. NMR, 1982.

81 (*overleaf*) Unloading bricks – obviously a common commodity on the river (*cf.* Pl. 35). H.W. Taunt, *c.*1895. Copyright Oxfordshire County Libraries.

TEDDINGTON LOCK.
The pound lock was opened in 1811 and still
marks the end of the tidal reach of the river
Thames. A foot-bridge, replacing the ferry, was
built to designs by G. Pooley in 1888-9. In fact
there are two bridges of different designs meeting
on the island. The materials were re-used from
the temporary bridge constructed at Hammersmith in 1884 and removed in 1887.

82 The bridge from the Surrey bank to the island.
NMR, 1980.

83, 84 (*below and overleaf*) The bridge from the
Middlesex bank to the island. NMR, 1980.

INDEX

References in roman numerals refer to introduction pages. Other references refer to the plates.